THE END OF THE ROAD

Ayn Rand

The End Of The Road

Ayn Rand presents her views of the world, politics, and human thought. Episode One focuses on the political state in America including Lyndon Johnson and McCarthy. BROADCAST: WBAI, 4 Apr. 1968.

THE END OF THE ROAD

THE END OF THE ROAD

Let us take a look at the Democratic Party.

It is only philosophical principles that enable men to look ahead, to project or plan the course of a country long range, in terms of years or decades. Today's disintegration has shrunk our vision to the range of a week or of a moment. What can one say about President Johnson's gesture of a renunciation, of refusing to run for the presidency?

One may regard it as melodrama or as sparse with equal validity. If it were fiction, one would say it is bad, improbable melodrama. One would say that no responsible statesman would announce such a momentous decision in such a manner, that he would not spring it on the country as a surprise, like a ham actor playing to a bored galley.

But this was not fiction. It was reality, the reality of today. The spectacle of the president of the greatest country on Earth announcing a decision that might affect the life of every human being in the world, a president concerned with the fact that the news had not leaked out, his manner suggesting pleasure in some thought such as: I stunned them, didn't I?

THE END OF THE ROAD

It is impossible to tell what President Johnson's future plans and intentions really are, but for the moment, what are we now left with in the Democratic Party? The Senators Eugene McCarthy and Robert Kennedy.

Both these gentlemen have recently written guest columns for the New York Times expressing their spiritual, intellectual positions. And they did it express it very eloquently, if you know how to read between the lines. I quote from the column by Senator McCarthy on March 30th, 1968.

THE END OF THE ROAD

Quote: "Everywhere I have campaigned, I have sensed a deep uneasiness about the war and about the quality of our leadership. It flows from a profound and growing conviction that something is wrong with the direction of American society. Americans are not by nature a people that wishes to oppress their fellow citizens or oppress the peoples of other nations, and they do not wish to be lead by fear. Yet, we see the growth of leadership by fear. We are finding among ourselves fear of remote enemies and fear of our fellow citizens.

THE END OF THE ROAD

"I have found this uneasiness among every kind of American, and my most urgent appeal is not any ready-made political bloc or alliance of interest or constituency in this country. It is to one constituency - a constituency of conscious, of hope and of trust in the future. Those who have come over to my cause have abandoned fear, disillusionment, defeatism and a kind of despair in America." Close quote.

THE END OF THE ROAD

What kind of fear is Senator McCarthy referring to? He does not specify. The column does not contain a single indication of who are the remote enemies or our own fellow citizens which Americans now fear, but surely, the implication is clear. It can only mean communism abroad and at home. Our remote enemies are the communists, the bloc of communist countries which has openly announced that they intend to conquer the world, and which, in the years since World War II, have been steadily enlarging their conquest of the world and have been gaining victories with our silent sanction by default. Is this what we are not supposed to fear?

THE END OF THE ROAD

If you see a horde of savages advancing upon you who have previously announced that they intend to exterminate and enslave you, wouldn't in reason be justified in feeling fear? Not the fear of cowardice, but the realization of the danger and the necessity of taking action against it. And if you see among your fellow citizens men who openly declare that their allegiance belongs to that savage horde, that they are communists or fellow travelers or sympathizers of communism and that they intend to enslave the rest of us, isn't that cause for feeling fear? Again, not the fear of cowardice, but the rational fear of realizing that one is up against a deadly enemy and that the battle is serious, that it is not to be solved by hope and trust but by clear policy and a consistent philosophy, including immoralities that opposes evil of that kind firmly, fearlessly and self-righteously.

But that is not what Senator McCarthy advocates. I do not mean to imply that the war in Vietnam is the proper way to fight communism. It is a useless, senseless war, which one should oppose not for the reasons offered by McCarthy or Kennedy, but by reason of the fact that it is a suicidal war which does not represent American national self-interest and in which America has nothing to gain.

However, Mr. McCarthy's program is not concerned merely with the war in Vietnam. He is talking in wider terms. And this man, who is now being publicized and acclaimed as a brave crusader, has nothing better to offer us in the face of today's world situation - nothing better than a few tired, old, benevolent bromides about hope and trust rather than fear, disillusionment, despotism and a kind of despair in America.

THE END OF THE ROAD

America today has good ground to feel despair, and one of these grounds is the fact that Senator McCarthy may claim, even for the moment, the position of a brave crusader if this is all that he has to offer. Senator McCarthy, however, is an almost appealing figure by comparison with his immediate rival, Senator Robert F. Kennedy. I quote from the column by Mr. Kennedy on February 10th, 1968.

Quote: "President Johnson speaks of a mood of restlessness. Cabinet officers and commentators, poets and protestors tell us that America is deep in a malaise of dispirit, discouraging initiative, paralyzing will and action. We have fought great wars, made unprecedented sacrifices at home and abroad, made prodigious efforts to achieve personal and national wealth, yet we ourselves are uncertain of what we have achieved and whether we like it.

"Our gross national product now soars over $800 billion a year, yet the gross national product does not allow for the health of our youth, the quality of their education, or the joy of their play. It does not include the beauty of our poetry or the strength of our marriages, the intelligence of our public debate, or the integrity of our public officials. It measures neither our wit nor our courage, neither our wisdom nor our learning, neither our compassion nor our devotion to country.

"It measures everything, in short, except that which makes life worthwhile, and it can tell us everything about America except why we are proud to be Americans." Close quote.

THE END OF THE ROAD

I should like to state at this point that it does tell me why I am proud to be an American, as it should be clear to everyone who knows where American achievement comes from and what enormous spiritual, intellectual heroism it represents.

Material wealth is not achieved by brute force. It is achieved by human intelligence. It is achieved by the thought and labor of free men - men living in a free country, men who are not enslaved and ordered by the state. America's material wealth is the physical symbol and result and product of the greatest spiritual, moral, heroic stature that mankind has ever seen in history, the stature of a country which for the first and only time in history had been built at least in part, at least fundamentally, on the concept of man's inalienable right to exist, on the concept of respect for man's individual rights.

American wealth, unmatched anywhere on Earth, is the result of that philosophy. That is what Americans are and should be proud of. And they should ask themselves, isn't it about time to stop attacking America for her greatest virtue, her wealth and her productive power? To stop apologizing for America's achievement by comparing her to the starving hordes of mankind on all other continents ruled by the philosophy of mysticism, altruism and collectivism which is now encroaching upon this country? Isn't it time to check our national premises and to take pride in the philosophy which made us great?

Not according to Senator Kennedy. To continue quoting from his column:
"America cannot act as if no other nation existed, flaunting our power and wealth against the judgment and desires of neutrals and likes alike. We wonder if we still hold the decent respect to the opinions of mankind or whether, like Athens of old, we will forfeit sympathy and support alike and ultimately our own security in the single-minded

pursuit of our own goals and objectives." Close quote.

I would like you to consider very literally and very carefully these particular words - "the single-minded pursuit of our own goals and objectives." Whose goals and objectives are we supposed to pursue? This is an almost explicit declaration that America should become the slave, serf and unpaid servant, the sacrificial animal to the needs of the rest of the world. By what right and for what reason?

THE END OF THE ROAD

For the reason that the rest of the world is perishing of envy of American power and therefore is entitled to our unrewarded self-sacrifice, to our health and our wealth, whereas we Americans are not entitled to any rights nor to the product of our own effort nor even to our lives. Why? Because we have achieved that which the whole world envies. And this is Senator Kennedy stating the essence, the philosophical base of his position.

And these, McCarthy and Kennedy, are the two leaders who allegedly have attracted the allegiance of American youth - of college students in particular - as representatives of a new, brave revolutionary movement. How new is it? It is only the stale, old, worn-out bromides of altruism and collectivism. That line is not the voice of the so-called establishment. That line is much, much older. Its roots are as old as the anti-man, anti-mind, anti-reason tradition of self-sacrifice, mysticism and tribal collectivism.

THE END OF THE ROAD

Here are some of the contemporary voices proclaiming that tradition explicitly. Here are the roots of which the Senators McCarthy and Kennedy are merely the branches, the small branches and the consequences. I quote from the New York Times of December 26, 1967.

"Pope Paul wished the world true peace and true happiness in contrast to mere pleasure and Dolce Vita in his Christmas message to the city and the world today. Too often, the pontiff said, modern man confuses happiness with a frenzy of happiness, of intensity, of enjoyment or of carefree living" - "Dolce Vita," the title of the famous Italian film in the pope's Italian text - "and with mere pleasure, satiety of earthly fulfillment and hedonistic well being." Close quote.

In other words, a frenzy of happiness, of intensity, of enjoyment, of carefree living is evil. Man should not aim at earthly fulfillment nor even at well being. Man should not seek happiness on Earth. He should sacrifice himself. Who, then, should enjoy the product of his earthly effort? Well, of course, those who have not achieved it. Should they rise and be able to achieve, they will no longer be entitled to any earthly fulfillment. We should all strive, struggle, sacrifice and perish, but never enjoy our life on Earth. This is a very ancient and very profound philosophical line.

But how could one make man accept such a horror, and why have men accepted it for centuries? Here is one of the indications of the reason. I quote from the New York Times of September 30, 1967.

"The pope spoke of immense danger caused by the irreligious orientation of the modern mentality. One error, the pope said, is to believe that one can forget orthodoxy and select only those truths that appeal to individual conscience and intellect. Another, he said, is that it is possible to give the faith new ideological dimensions other than those outlined by genuine tradition. Faith is a mysterious gift which demands docility and responsiveness." Close quote.

It is not difficult to see at what enemy this type of statement is directed. The enemy is man's mind, man's independent reasoning, man's individual conscience. Man should not exercise it, according to this school of thought. They should give in their intellectual freedom in order to practice faith, docility and responsiveness.

THE END OF THE ROAD

That line is not confined to the Catholic Church. A new study in the New York Times of October 7, 1967 reported the following. Quote:

"Ministers warned that unless the churches offered biblically sanctioned supernatural experiences, people would increasingly turn to spiritualist practices or drugs such as LSD for a sense of relief from mundane existence. Young people today are simply craving for visions, so they turn to LSD in order to get that trip out of the bondage to human limitations. They are participants in what is broadly termed 'the charismatic movement,' which emphasizes supernatural manifestations such as praying in unknown towns, unpremeditated prophecy said to be utterance inspired by the holy spirit, and healing - all reputedly common in the ancient Christian Church." Close quote.

This is how the modern movement is. One can quite agree with this last statement. The choice is between mystical, supernatural faith or LSD - except that it is truly not much of a choice. Both phenomena belong to the same side, to the rebellion against man's mind.

THE END OF THE ROAD

This is what is offered to the youth of today as a new, modern, progressive, rebellious trend. If it is a rebellion, it is a rebellion against man and against man's mind. It is the blind alley, the dead end of altruism, collectivism and mysticism in the modern world.

The newspapers reported that college students celebrated the news of President Johnson's renunciation with cries of, We are saved! We are saved! They meant, apparently, their hope for the end of the war in Vietnam and their salvation from the fate of sacrificial animals to the military draft. The pathetic and tragic element of their celebration is that they did not realize that we're supporting and endorsing the very principles that had made Vietnam and the draft possible: the abolition of individual rights, the enslavement of the individual to the totalitarian state - the welfare state.

Who, then, are to be the rebels and the standard bearers of the future? One does not rebel by being more royalist than the king or more altruist in today's establishment. An actual rebellion has to challenge basic premises. The rebels and the standard bearers of the future are those who have the courage to advocate reason, capitalism and man's individual rights and man's right to exist for his own sake.

THE END OF THE ROAD

It is not too late. That battle and that rebellion are barely beginning. But that is what the world needs today and is waiting for. And if the world is to have a future, then it is the rebellion of man, of man's self-esteem, of man's reason against the perishing altruist, collectivist, mystic axis that will give the world its future and its freedom.

Recommended Readings

• Siddhartha by Hermann Hesse, www.bnpublishing.net

•The Anatomy of Success, Nicolas Darvas, www.bnpublishing.net

• The Dale Carnegie Course on Effective Speaking, Personality Development, and the Art of How to Win Friends & Influence People, Dale Carnegie, www.bnpublishing.net

• The Law of Success In Sixteen Lessons by Napoleon Hill (Complete, Unabridged), Napoleon Hill, www.bnpublishing.net

• It Works, R. H. Jarrett, www.bnpublishing.net

- The Art of Public Speaking (Audio CD), Dale Carnegie, wwww.bnpublishing.net

- The Success System That Never Fails (Audio CD), W. Clement Stone, www.bnpublishing.net

THE END OF THE ROAD

NOTES

NOTES

NOTES

NOTES

NOTES